D0912937

All-Time Sports Records

EXTREME SPORTS RECORDS

MARK WEAKLAND

BLACK
RABBIT
BOOKS

Bolt is published by Black Rabbit Books
P.O. Box 3263, Mankato, Minnesota, 56002.
www.blackrabbitbooks.com
Copyright © 2021 Black Rabbit Books

Jen Besel, editor; Catherine Cates, designer;
Omay Ayres, photo researcher

Library of Congress Cataloging-in-Publication Data
Names: Weakland, Mark, author.
Title: Extreme sports records / by Mark Weakland.
Other titles: Bolt (North Mankato, Minn.)
Description: Mankato, Minnesota : Black Rabbit Books, 2021. | Series: Bolt.
All-time sports records | Includes webography. |
Audience: Ages: 8-12 years. | Audience: Grades: 4-6.
Identifiers: LCCN 2019027449 (print) | ISBN 9781623102401 (Hardcover) |
ISBN 9781644663363 (Paperback) | ISBN 9781623103347 (eBook)
Subjects: LCSH: Extreme sports—Records—Juvenile literature. |
Extreme sports—History—Juvenile literature. | Athletes—Rating of.
Classification: LCC GV749.7 .W33 2021 (print) | LCC GV749.7 (ebook) |
DDC 796.04/6—dc23
LC record available at https://lccn.loc.gov/2019027449
LC ebook record available at https://lccn.loc.gov/2019027450

Printed in the United States. 2/20

All records and statistics are current as of 2019.

CONTENTS

CHAPTER 1

Live

EXTREME

Someone in a **kayak** hurtles over a waterfall. Another person climbs a towering cliff without a rope. Extreme sports athletes are skillful and brave. Some of their records are so amazing, they might never be broken.

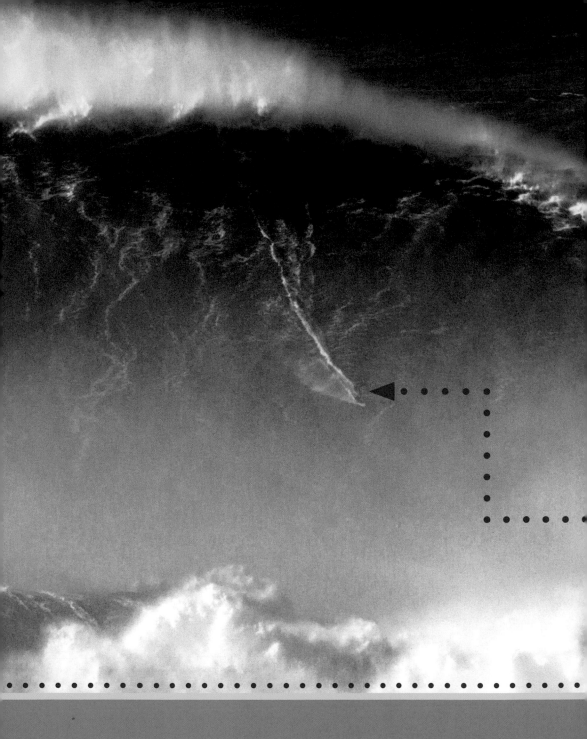

Breaking records takes hard work. **Verifying** those records is hard too. Officials in each sport talk to witnesses. They look at video and photos. They measure speed and distance. Then they decide if a record was set.

CHAPTER 2

Unbelievable

RECORD!

Tallest Wave Ever Surfed **80 FEET** (24 meters)

Surfing an ocean wave takes a lot of skill. It takes nerves of steel when the wave is 80 feet (24 m) tall. Surfer Rodrigo Koxa faced that mighty wave in 2017. He set a world record.

RECORD!
Fastest Time by a Female to Ride around the World on a Bicycle **152 DAYS, 1 HOUR**

In 2012, Juliana Buhring did what few people have ever done. She rode a bicycle the **circumference** of the earth. And she did it faster than any other female before. On her bike, nicknamed Pegasus, she traveled through 18 countries. She did it in just over 152 days.

STARTING AND ENDING POINT

RULES!

TO SET THIS RECORD, BUHRING HAD TO FOLLOW THESE RULES.

TRAVEL AT LEAST 24,900 MILES (40,073 KILOMETERS) IN ONE DIRECTION

START AND END IN THE SAME PLACE

TRAVEL BY SEA AND AIR WAS ALLOWED, BUT AT LEAST 18,000 MILES (28,968 KM) OF THE ROUTE HAD TO BE RIDDEN ON A BIKE

9

RECORD!

Highest Waterfall Navigated in a Kayak **189.5 FEET** (58 m)

The Palouse Falls in Washington state is impressive. It has a nearly 200-foot (61-m) drop. At least 1,000 cubic feet (28 cubic meters) of water pours over the edge each second. Tyler Brandt kayaked the falls in 2009. And he survived!

• •

It took Brandt 3.7 seconds to plummet down the falls. He reached a falling speed of at least 100 miles (161 km) per hour.

RECORD!
Deepest Cave Dive **927 FEET** (283 m)

The bottom of Boesmansgat Cave in South Africa is 927 feet (283 m) down. No one but Nuno Gomes has ever been to the bottom. In 1996, Gomes dove down in the darkness. It took 15 minutes to get to the bottom. But it took 12 hours to come back up. He had to come up very slowly to avoid **decompression sickness**. When he surfaced, he held the record for deepest cave dive.

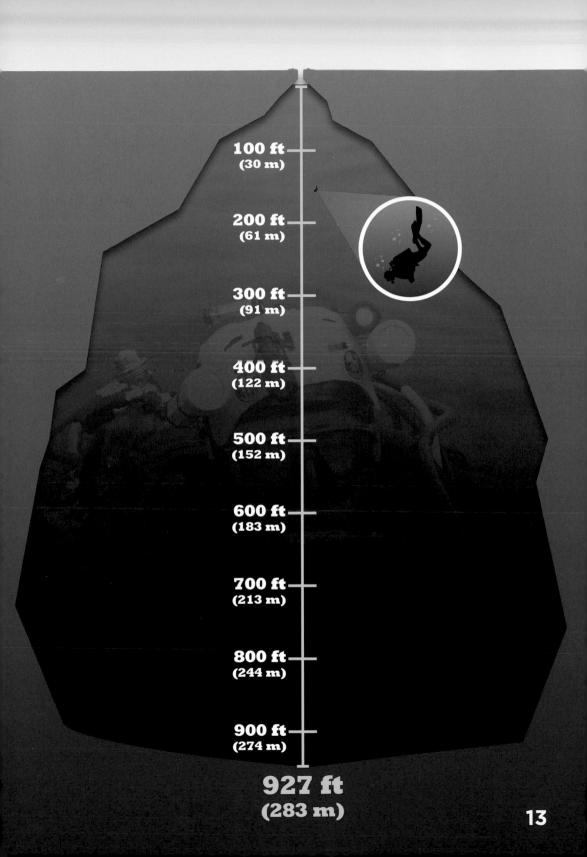

100 ft
(30 m)

200 ft
(61 m)

300 ft
(91 m)

400 ft
(122 m)

500 ft
(152 m)

600 ft
(183 m)

700 ft
(213 m)

800 ft
(244 m)

900 ft
(274 m)

927 ft
(283 m)

13

14

RECORD!

Highest Jump on a BMX Bike **27 FEET** (8.23 m)

BMX bike riders rely on skill and power to do their tricks. They bounce down steps. They rocket off steep ramps. BMX rider Kevin Robinson flew into the world record books. He soared 27 feet (8.23 m) above the top of a quarter pipe ramp. That's 54 feet (16 m) off the ground.

BMX High Air Records
(Off a Quarter Pipe Ramp)

Kevin Robinson	Mat Hoffman	Morgan Wade
27 feet	**26.5 feet**	**23.9 feet**
(8.23 m)	(8.08 m)	(7.28 m)

RECORD!
Highest Free Solo Climb **3,000 FEET** (914 m)

Free soloing is extremely dangerous. Climbers **scale** rock cliffs with nothing but their hands and feet. They have no spikes to grab. They have no ropes to hold. Alex Honnold has the world record in free soloing. He climbed a rock wall 3,000 feet (914 m) high.

RECORD!

Highest Fixed Object for Bungee Jumping **1,053 FEET** (321 m)

Bungee jumpers leap off fixed objects, such as bridges and cliffs. They can also jump from movable objects like helicopters. The world's highest fixed object bungee jump is 1,053 feet (321 m) high.

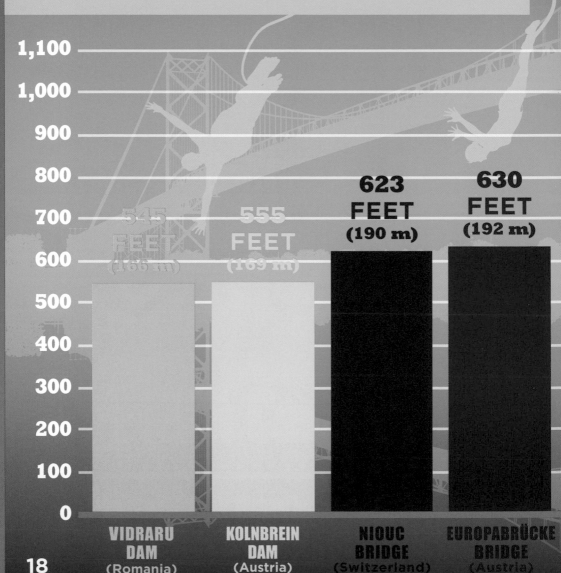

	545 FEET (166 m)	555 FEET (169 m)	623 FEET (190 m)	630 FEET (192 m)
	VIDRARU DAM (Romania)	KOLNBREIN DAM (Austria)	NIOUC BRIDGE (Switzerland)	EUROPABRÜCKE BRIDGE (Austria)

18

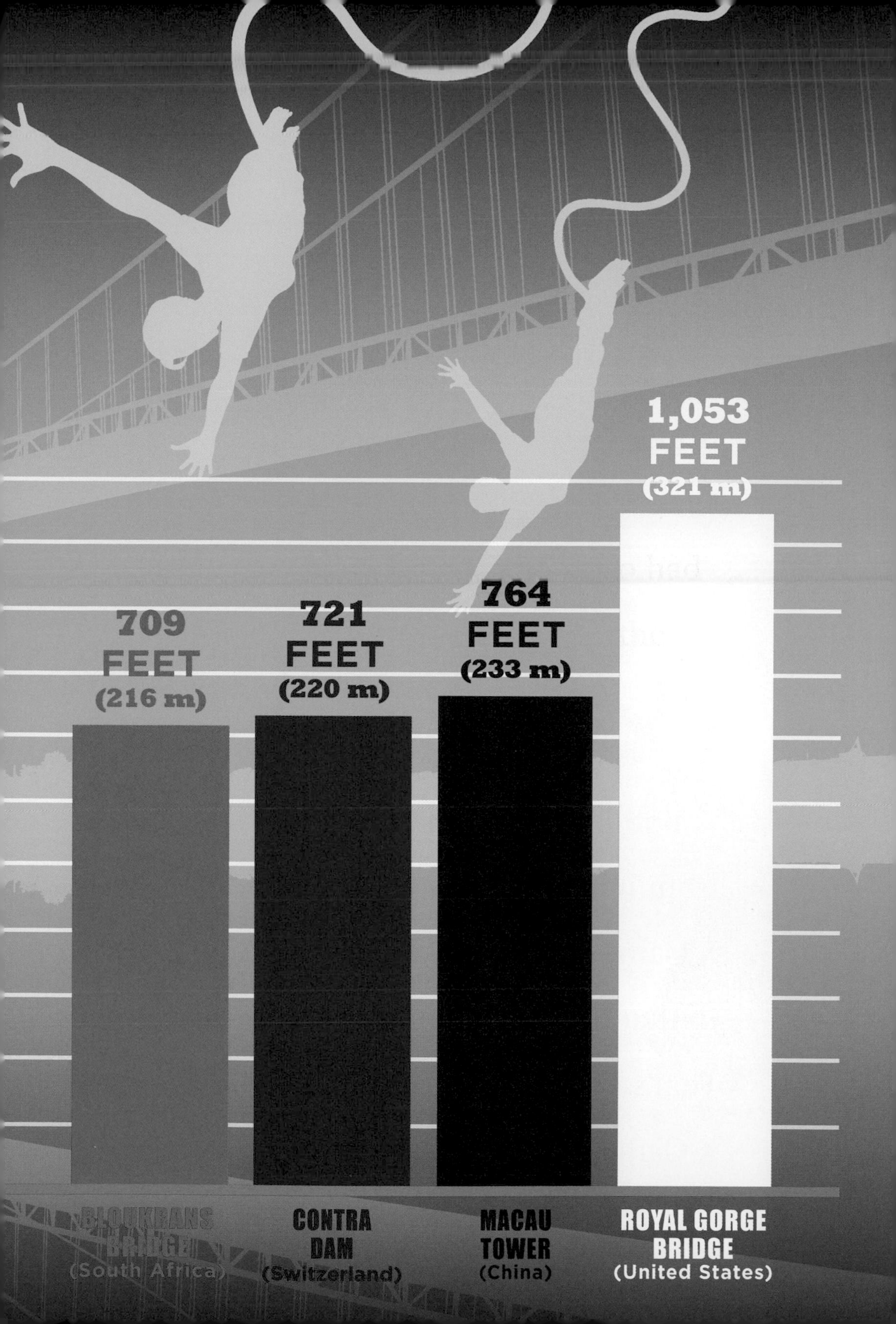

709 FEET (216 m)

721 FEET (220 m)

764 FEET (233 m)

1,053 FEET (321 m)

BLOUKRANS BRIDGE (South Africa)

CONTRA DAM (Switzerland)

MACAU TOWER (China)

ROYAL GORGE BRIDGE (United States)

RECORD!

Most Individual Men's Career X Games Medals **30**

Bob Burnquist is a skateboarder from Brazil. He competed in the X Games between 1997 and 2015. In that time, he earned 30 medals. That's more than any other X Games athlete.

20

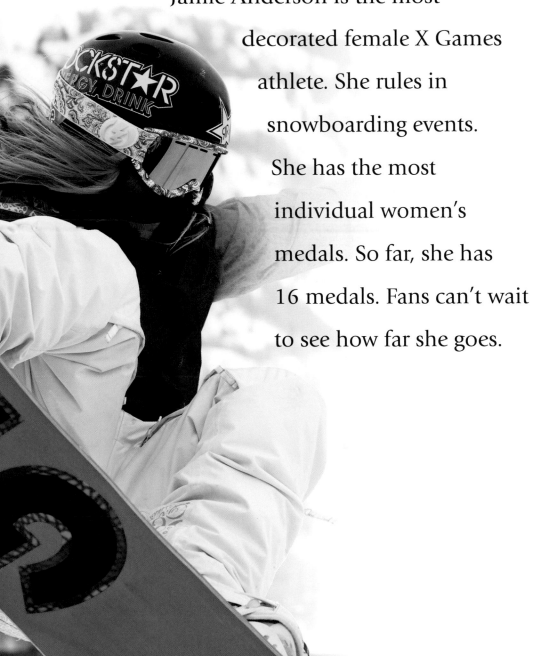

RECORD!
Most Individual Women's Career X Games Medals 16

Jamie Anderson is the most decorated female X Games athlete. She rules in snowboarding events. She has the most individual women's medals. So far, she has 16 medals. Fans can't wait to see how far she goes.

21

RECORD!
Farthest Flight by a Wingsuit Flier
18.26 MILES (29 kilometers)

Wingsuit fliers are like flying squirrels. But they don't leap from trees. They jump off bridges and cliffs. They even jump from airplanes. Andy Stumpf holds the record for longest wingsuit flight. He jumped out of a plane at about 36,000 feet (10,973 m) up. He then flew more than 18 miles (29 km).

RECORD!

Age of Youngest Athlete to Finish an Ironman Race **14**

Ironman races are some of the toughest races in the world. Athletes swim 2.4 miles (3.9 km). Then they bike 112 miles (180 km). At the end, they run about 26 miles (42 km).

In 1982, Rodkey Faust became the youngest person to finish it. He was 14 years old. He finished in less than 14 hours.

RECORD!

Fastest Finish Time in the World's Longest Footrace

40 DAYS, 9 HOURS, 6 SECONDS

The longest footrace in the world is a race around the block. But runners have to go around the block 5,649 times! The 3,100-mile (4,989-km) race is held in New York each year. In 2016, Ashprihanal Aalto ran the race in about 40 days.

25

EXTREME SPORTS RECORDS

BY THE NUMBERS

11 FEET, 5 INCHES (3.5 M)
HIGHEST JUMP ON A POGO STICK
(BIFF HUTCHISON)

91 YEARS, 189 DAYS
age of oldest person to paraglide
(JANUSZ ORLOWSKI)

16.3 MILES (26 KM) distance of longest wheelie in a wheelchair (Xie Junwu)

164 ft (50 m) in **8.55 SECONDS** SPEED RECORD IN HAND SKATING (MIRKO HANBEN)

CHAPTER 3

Can It Get More EXTREME?

Extreme sports athletes push the limits. They want to climb higher and fall faster. They want to run farther and dive deeper. The more they push, the harder the records are to break.

GLOSSARY

decompression sickness (dee-kum-PREH-shun SIK-nus)—a dangerous condition caused by bubbles which form in the blood and other body parts of people who have the pressure around them decrease too quickly

circumference (sur-KUM-frens)—the distance around something

kayak (KI-ak)—a small boat that is pointed at both ends, holds one or two people, and is moved by a paddle with two blades

paraglide (PAR-uh-glid)—the recreational sport of soaring from a slope or a cliff using a modified parachute

scale (SKAYL)—to climb

verify (VEHR-uh-fy)—to confirm or establish truth or accuracy

wingsuit (WING-soot)—a jumpsuit with folds of fabric between the arms and legs that create lift when extended and allow the wearer to glide through the air over long distances

BOOKS

Beer, Julie, and Michelle Harris. *Extreme Records: The Tallest, Weirdest, Fastest, Coolest Stuff on Planet Earth.* National Geographic Kids. Washington, D.C.: National Geographic, 2018.

Hawkes, Chris, Scarlett O'Hara, Fleur Star, eds. *Record Breakers!* New York: DK Publishing, 2018.

O'Brien, Cynthia. *Scholastic Book of World Records 2018.* New York: Scholastic Inc., 2017.

WEBSITES

10 Extreme Sports Guinness World Records
planetairsports.com/10-extreme-guiness-world-records/

42 Breathtaking Facts about Extreme Sports
www.factinate.com/things/42-facts-extreme-sports/

X Games
www.xgames.com

INDEX